I WILL SAY BEAUTY

I WILL SAY BEAUTY
CAROL FROST

TRIQUARTERLY BOOKS
NORTHWESTERN UNIVERSITY PRESS
EVANSTON, ILLINOIS

TriQuarterly Books
Northwestern University Press
Evanston, Illinois 60208-4210

Copyright © 2003 by Carol Frost. Published 2003 by TriQuarterly Books/Northwestern
University Press. All rights reserved.

Printed in the United States of America

10 9 8 7 6 5 4 3 2 1

ISBN 0-8101-5138-3 (cloth)
ISBN 0-8101-5139-1 (paper)

LIBRARY OF CONGRESS CATALOGING-IN-PUBLICATION DATA

Frost, Carol, 1948–
  I will say beauty / Carol Frost.
    p. cm.
    ISBN 0-8101-5138-3 (alk. paper) — ISBN 0-8101-5139-1 (pbk. : alk. paper)
    1. Nature—Poetry. I. Title.
  PS3556.R596 I18 2003
  813'.54—dc21

                                                        2002154637

For Tom and Carolyn Tucker

Beauty is but a flower,
Which wrinkles will devour;
Brightness falls from the air . . .
　　—Thomas Nashe, "Song in Time of Pestilence"

Who cares if you come from paradise or hell,
Appalling Beauty . . .
　　　—Charles Baudelaire, "Hymn to Beauty"

. . . the sea's huge gaiety . . .
　　　—Charles Baudelaire, "Obsession"

Contents

Acknowledgments xi

Winter Without Snow 2
Wet Spring Day 3

ONE

Gull 7
"Four Serious Songs, Opus 121" 8
Water Lyrics 10
Inlet 11

TWO

Wild Rose 15
Ardors 16
The Part of the Bee's Body Embedded in the Flesh 17

THREE

Sunrise 21
The Mysterious Quality of Enchantment 22
Driftwood 23

FOUR

Windows 27
Foxes 28
Fence Wire 30
Martin's Summer 31

FIVE

Nature Has 35
Whelks 36
Moon 37

SIX

Lying in the Pollen and Water 41
Thunderstorm 42
Star-Gazer Lilies 43

SEVEN

Paradise 47
Kayaking after Dusk 49
Given 50

EIGHT

Reap 53
How to Hunt 54
Mr. Brink 55

NINE

Conch 59
Rays 60
Requin 62

TEN

Eel Spearing 67
The Gross Clinic 69
Apiary IX 71

ELEVEN

A Woman like Yourself 75
Hem of Sunlight 76
Hydrangeas 78
One Fine Day 79

Acknowledgments

Many thanks to the editors of the journals where these poems first appeared:

AGNI: "Requin" and "Thunderstorm"

Gettysburg Review: "Moon" and "Water Lyrics"

Green Mountains Review: "Reap" and "Whelks"

Kenyon Review: "Gull" and "Driftwood"

Lyric: "Martin's Summer" and "The Part of the Bee's Body Embedded in the Flesh"

Marlboro Review: "Given," "Mr. Brink," and "The Mysterious Quality of Enchantment"

Michigan Quarterly Review: "Sunrise"

New England Review: "How to Hunt," "Inlet," and "Windows"

Northwest Review: "Conch"

Paris Review: "Ardors" and "Fence Wire"

Prairie Schooner: "Lying in the Pollen and Water," "Wet Spring Day," and "Wild Rose"

Sewanee Theological Review: "Hem of Sunlight"

Southern Review: "'Four Serious Songs, Opus 121,'" "Paradise," "A Woman like Yourself," "The Gross Clinic," and "Hydrangeas"

TriQuarterly: "Kayaking after Dusk" and "Nature Has"

Valparaiso Review: "One Fine Day"

"Eel Spearing" first appeared in *Contemporary Poetry of New England,* edited by Robert Pack and Jay Parini (University Press of New England). "Requin" also appeared in *Hammer and Blaze,* edited by Heather McHugh and Ellen Bryant Voigt (University of Georgia Press). "The Part of the Bee's Body Embedded in the Flesh" was selected for *The Pushcart Prize XXVII.*

Thanks to Hartwick College and to the Hartwick College trustees for a writing grant and to the Ledig Rohwhalt Foundation for the residency at Château de Lavigny, where I completed work on this book.

Most of all, thanks to Richard Frost for his belief in my poems and for his laughter.

I WILL SAY BEAUTY

The man carried bucket after bucket of plaster dust
up the earthen ramp of the barn that caught fire
and emptied each as if he were dumping snow
onto the blackened beams.
In the trees there were little glass seeds,
souvenirs of winter without snow.

When the man turned back toward the house,
he wore a helmet of dusty mother-of-pearl
and his eyelashes were silvery half-moons.
I watched him with all the coldness I had,
yet it would not snow.

Nothing could make it snow.
Not the burst water pipes, the leggings,
the sleds, or the white horses.
Not the smoky fountains, the clouds.
They were souvenirs of winter without snow,
as was my wish for a white field
like a fresh beginning.

Wet Spring Day

A spring day like this how yellow the air is, a sea, spars
plump with flowers and leaves and the ground soaked,
the robins ravenous, splashing in the flood, plucking
between pokeweed and grass blade the attenuated wet
worm. Where is the keel, the ballast, the configuration
of older stars to keep us on course? The watery path
searching a way; the silken web winking in the wet sun-
light:—After winter, the earth and water are fabulous,
the wind shakes out the pollen sails,
and we could nearly lose ourselves. It could be like waking
from a cold dream, boxes of snow, and cadging sense, to the yellow
and green textures, the sun-drenched southern reaches
of thought, off charts, passionate as seraphim, pure as
water, salty, billowing.

ONE

Every wing, every instant burgeoning with wind,

has an attendant grace. The sky sweats, copper

haze blears the horizon for tomorrow's storm

the gulls annunciate. Ah (you say), also consider

the flesh of the turtle burnt black by strange

decay—turnips gone bad crowding the air—

and the hoarse whispers of the sea,

Icarus consumed in the burning sea. Wild

honey drowned, nymphs, empty cans, plastic

flip-flops, boats broken from their moorings,

capsized, all are pulled down. Who rises?

Gulls steel their wings, their cries hardly

angelic, bruiting changes in weather,

but I have seen them make of struggle

an arrow, a silken figure, and a plumb bob,

whatever was needed while the winds clocked,

as if *if* they were miraculously related

to time, the storm would blow itself out.

Natural enough, that, but no less

beautiful, stopping in flight, racing, their breasts

now pink, now yellow in fallen sunlight.

"Four Serious Songs, Opus 121"

Beautifully and elliptically the sunlight plays
on the syllables of the sea a few small songs
of morning, and the herring gulls rise
in swirling sixths, then descend in thirds,
not that it is that way, *yucca-yucca, yucca-*
yucca is their sound, but the light gray backs and wings
catch the light and swirl of May and morning,
and I am again in Vienna, a Brahms air in mind.
The day Brahms wrote *Vier ernste Gesänge*
he ordered a new coat from his tailor. Remorseless,
a friend who'd lost his wife called the new music
and thanked Brahms. "O Tod, O Tod,"
the third song opens, four half notes
for a bass voice, yet in the bitter valedictory
the composer's *Engel* speak of moonlight, and dark
burnished sonorities disclose how once for music
having left the world, Brahms never would turn back, never
did. He composed the songs on his birthday,
and I can almost see him at the ebony piano
singing through his breath, humming. It was his living,
but much more. On a May morning, consider
too his jaundice and dying, he contrived and daydreamed
and sang scale fragments and words as simple as cattle
of our bearing up. Really, it's like these gulls
whose flight enters the body, the short life
inland, the vast skies, wing ache; then it's hard
not to imagine Brahms' own shoulders slumping.
He apologized often for his dark moods
and wrote of his "loveliest melodies" to Clara Schumann
that they were hers. "If I think of myself, nothing
clever, let alone beautiful, could occur to me."
But he marked down more notes, squaring

his shoulders again, the May breeze a breathy sweetness
sliding under the sill and a portent. The lindens
would again be bare. He tinkered, taking notes
from the *C-sharp Minor Intermezzo,* quoting himself
and others, waiting for his tailor—a day so composed
of ordinary events it means everything. The gulls,
now, stand on the little archipelago of sand
the tide with its two minds has given them, and are silent.
"Dann geht dem Menschen wie dem Vieh,"
the composer said and ten months later, in pencil
to his mother, "For the sake of a change I have lain down,"
his last melodies feasting on melody like old starlight
on water, sunshine having honeycombed the end of day.

Water Lyrics

High tide at last; and waters spread
across the marsh like the shadow
of a great tree, the wind gone dead.

Nothing stirs until it stirs—
a mullet, egret, or the breeze
freshening. Tide turns. A few birds

lift from wrinkling limbs, showing how
the next minute and morning
comes, and dusk, and the shape of things.

The band of sunshine

leading west grows more narrow

and still more golden

on the gulf while the evening

breeze winds its transparent way

the old nets swirling

by pilings were once tresses

for goddesses. Gulls

call through the morning: not grief,

not pain, not anxious fearing

Wherever tidal
waters slow, they drop sand and
mark a contour where
other waters slow. I say
love and hate come on this way.

As you enter, groping, the channel
waters show the way, shallows
prickling, jagged oyster
mounds beneath the great supple
skin of the tide, fruit of the sea
the tribes harvested before Spanish horses
sank to the belly in back bayou. You drift,
boat nodding,
to the island's interior.
No sound, no sound, then a very small slur
from a spoonbill, and you are more
alone than ever,
more than anyone ever, perhaps. Except,
except for the lob-tailing mullet—
there!—and the bird. You will not forget
its slur and trill. All done now.
If absence breeds presence—
I refuse to explain further—
you may want to drift for days through this
teeming place—salted meadows,
immense surfaces of one inch
deep waters,
cedars, herons, bald eagles, palms.
Remember the tide
dragging back shreds of itself,
and go now; take nothing; already too much
time has slid by.
Paddle quickly through the narrows.
See? At the entrance to the gulf
a raccoon is standing, his small hands empty.

TWO

Wild Rose

Shall I perfect myself or ramble? The arbor's crumbled
and no one comes to brush the spiders from my petals.
I dislike their pursed and little mouths,
but they can bear themselves aloft.
Umbrels and sconces are vanities,
and if I fold myself in quarters
and anchor to the barn's foundation,
I can stick my face into darkness
and be all the wiser, the spiders say
in all but words. I know winter's dark,
a faded tint of apricot and purple letting go
in surface layers of softest snow
above; and that becomes the greenery I waken to.
For such darkness I must only wait,
but I'll freely search wherever a little loam and water
lie—the southern slopes, a sheltered hollow, this barn
corner—for the other. Only if the dark conceives it
must I think of beauty—my interiors, silks
there, and the looping quiet in the morning of the spiders.

Ardors

The tortoise walks on tiptoe in June,
the month of his ardors.
Buttery light, distant thunder
in the month of my ardors.

≈

Flailing boughs, coral lime
in the wind and verdure.
Then silence, dark creamy
shadows in nighttime verdure.

≈

The moon traversing the garden,
florals made of a blush or a breath,
nightbirds with a little lump
of insect under their tongues, breath

≈

of clover, grassy, spiced,
and all of it rinsed of emotion.
The leaden nymph by the gate.
All, all rinsed of emotion.

≈

By what bough are the fireflies
hidden, and the stars?
The night's leavings in daylight
lie hidden like the stars.

The Part of the Bee's Body Embedded in the Flesh

The bee-boy, *merops apiaster,* on sultry thundery days
filled his bosom between his coarse shirt and his skin
with bees—his every meal wild honey.
He had no apprehension of their stings or didn't mind
and gave himself—his palate, the soft tissues of his throat—
what Rubens gave to the sun's illumination
stealing like fingers across a woman's thigh
and van Gogh's brushwork heightened.
Whatever it means, why not say it hurts—
the mind's raw, gold coiling whirled against
air currents, want, and beauty? I *will* say beauty.

THREE

Sunrise

Tuesday's parchment with a gold seal,
no storm clouds, and the balletic birds performing
Gull Lake above the knife-bright shallows;
not birdwatching, really, I don't keep a list,
and my long glasses let in too little light,
but the tide ticks under the dock and birds swoop.
What next? The saw grass, rushes for Moses,
rushes for Leda, died back in a few days' cold,
but trout nose in still. The old laws, it seems,
still flower. The busy bee hums happy
in its vocation; red blossoms are everywhere.
They groan and laugh with the wind,
their scent mingling with the black-gold scent
of muck. I sprawl on a chaise, pig gold
orange spreading like an oil slick on the silent sea.
Stop that racket, less flapping; and diminuendo,
please; one less pirouette for life's salt and sweet
design, less beauty, less breakneck speed.

The Mysterious Quality of Enchantment

Skimmers nearly upon the sea's oily sequins,
pleated and blotted mudflats floating soon
with gold fans, and the dried lei of a snake, so hard
to bring oneself to touch, we walked together
at lowest tide. Heartless (who hasn't lost heart),
you turned aside, as a sleeper turns to the wall,
letting the body figure out on its own where it must be.
One can think about it, but then one has to sleep.
Then the seascape—blend of salt-wisp and mirror—
was too lovely to bear, or too lonely.
The massed ibises! Remember? When you gestured at them for me,
they rose like smoke, spread, and disappeared.

Driftwood

Have I lied to myself about art?
Everything can't be art. Bird not bird
but driftwood roughed up by the sea,
forgotten, found, by one who desires
a gnarled reminder of form, and flight.
I consider my own similes—gardens, trees,
an orchard still rooted, light marine
in the blown air, fruit drunken on the swirl,
like everything that leads up to a legend
of leaving. Poor driftwood, poor
bird, with your premise of wings.

FOUR

Windows

Without meaning to we stand at windows
then see another bird's ascent,
a sweet, negligent sentence

that the mind magnifies:
how a bunting comes to bear columns of air,

then in one small avalanche of glinting flight
anticipates all that has come and gone.

Couldn't we go, too?—into the autumn hemlocks,
along rivers, hills red-shawled, space spinning

and spinning through us,
so that what we've not known we knew

suddenly stretches and sets itself free—
irreversible curve—and is completely light.

Foxes

FOR BRIGIT KELLY

Only in forgetting map and compass
could they follow the fall
of the land and feel in the shiver of leaves
in beech and oak a moment's
tissue. They stood in ashes of shadows
and failing light, varying degrees
of decay beneath their feet—leafmeal, quill,
soft stones of dung—and breathed,
turning to look cold north, to the receding east,
south, and amber west. As for the drifting voices
up from the valley floor—a boy calling a dog,
a thumping car radio, the gravel and vibrato
of a distant train—those carried
farther than the ridge and were lost
somewhere in a thicket of thorn apples
or an old pasture closing in with birch.
All are lost, artifacts of what has gone
from a person's life, with some remnants
in a dreamscape—ribbons, bottles, wheels off toys,
a finger tracing the inside line of an ear,
ghostly, a smudge of smile, or someone's final kiss.
The woods are strange. Ferns cover barbed wire,
a Buick chassis lies upside down, crushed,
peppered with rust. In the rising darkness,
a fox runs through a clearing to a stream
and stands, fur lit pink-amber, to drink,
the only creature here who seems beyond confusion.
Soon it, too, will be gone or merely invisible
in the darkness coming on. And still
they linger, as if whatever is missing shall return,

bringing in its own coming its never-fading
and fading, as their friend told them
that by standing still in this field
at dusk, lost, they would see the foxes.

Fence Wire

. . . garroting apple and oak, broken off, no longer keeping the wild estate;
late spring, northern embroidery; lilies shaped like trumpets, chalices;
the names are royal: Imperial Crimson, Empress of China;
but deer eat the bulbs, turning from forage, leaping
the humming string set on wire sticks beside the compost and garden
lined with mothballs, urine, and lantern fires; the abandoned
woods still fill in around the double-wides, as though a wound
were closing, and the earth's chill shadows multiply . . . bits of wire
everywhere, fern fronds, skunks, daylilies, badgers
going along silently, and the unruled land goes along too,
bramble-wild, strung out, dowdy in rich or sere evening air . . .

Martin's Summer

Cold green parting
to admit us.

Mayapples, piccolo
piccolo birds, wings,
voices.

Water running
through such cool fingers.

Why speak when we can see
and breathe
the early gossamer, Love,
plumy, gray?

Later we'll say deer
walked near (sweet mire).
And this our keepsake:

the soft wind and the gate
after gate
we walked through

an evening, a quarter hour,
abbreviated melodies
somewhere above, rain,
then serer light.

We want but little more;
nor that *more* long.

FIVE

Nature Has

Nature has a sexual sense of humor. A bee swigs nectar, the tail
of a neighborhood cat lifts, a shawl of white blossoms wafts from
the apple tree onto the dirt, until a breeze tweaks an exposed place,
a bottom—storms of pollen and flitting laughter. What birds
are these? They are singing. *Sex in the wind, love in the trees, sex
in the grasses, eggs in the nest.* But yourself, surely more complex,
with your imaginary lives and your off-keyed moon, do you blush toward
the meeting in the bower, a lark fluent in the leaves,
soft fires underneath and the trilling
ruthless? The fallen angels love you and what they do to you—
your senses and little white lies and rampant heart.

Whelks

Numerous as figs, as bees, and susceptible to currents, whelks
move through the swirl, and people here pick them for food.
A handful's about ten, and they'll tickle when they try to slide on a pod
and mucous film back to the water, carrying their many-banded shell,
many-banded like the honeybee, black and gold and pearled with barnacles.
Tom says the tickling is sensual but odd; Holly drops her whelks at first touch,
the living fluids and stirring
flesh a horror in a thing so strange. Boiled, a whelk's a sweet bean on the tongue,
saline, as we are. You can taste the sea, its darkness, but also filtered sunlight,
and years of microbits of flora, a little sand.
Best just to go lightly: Swallow. Breathe. The shells are too small
to hold up to the ear, whatever wind spirals there too light to hear.
The body has a season and hungers.

Moon

Grief again, the turntable left on
and the needle set at the beginning
of our song before the rebuff, you gone

back to your life. The lopsided moon sings
outside on the trellis its style of song
and I can hear, ghostly, the little rhymes

that rhyme with *sad*. I haven't the heart
to close the blinds. They stay as they are left.
Shadows pile in the corners, a part

of the night, the speckled air adrift
and filling with the soft valley mist
for morning. I call it my season

for misery, like watching winter come,
cold rain blown, hardening into snow,
then lasting too long. When rain trickles from

the eaves, I'll go where least shadows
lie, moon-tossed, at garden end, a sparrow
in the tree with its three notes, and hear him.

SIX

Lying in the Pollen and Water

Lying in the pollen and water, muffled tones in the air, thinking
of the magical and savage passage of sunlight across a winter field,
across the faces of friends marred by disappointment or turned
regretful, and Mother's bronze dream of divinity, an escarpment of
clouds parting, four winds drumming, and being wrapped in warm
mists, set down again in my own perfumed childhood bedroom,
the simplicity like a tune of a few notes, whole notes, I watch
the white pillow of the apple tree, petals drifting on me, and I feel
my mind swerve, spring's malignity whispering and singing what
it knows and I've always known,—that I will be covered
over by snow, or stone, or light, or moldering dark, the body the grave,
its lineaments and fibers great and less, the details of a sort
of fermentation at the bottom of all sweetness (little hesitations
and abnegations, a late, pensive morning).

Thunderstorm

Poom, the sky says, then raking gales and huge yellow
and copper flowers, backlit, bearing no creases from having been folded
tightly in the bud. Each flash of lightning such a flower.

Only let the moments revolve, while petals pile around the glass door.
The ventriloquist is leaving. Listen. His doll,
somewhere behind in greenery, wants it to end, and to sit and speak

and open his wooden eyelids without someone's hand reaching
into his back. He practices and, from deep in his throat, a small rumble

comes, muffled, the sound a wood stick makes
dragging across wavy steel. What he means is nothing left to fear.

Star-Gazer Lilies

Where for this chemistry is there a greater beauty?
Already the hummingbirds are sucking sugar
and pepper, blossoms frail from such attention.
On what better silk does decay mingle with light,
each lapped device tremulous, loose?

SEVEN

Paradise

The porpoise arced through yellow glaze, a scimitar,
to breathe the humid air and plunge back into its wavy world,
the many-doored water, ajar in an offshore breeze.
And from the shore, those who looked with binoculars
to the closest key could see in a loblolly pine
two eagles, but not the bowled-over graveyard
or the stone foundations of the cedar pencil mills
hidden in the palms that whisper and clatter, green
and silver like immense seabirds standing on a single leg.
After the ferry lets you off—the *Island Hopper*—
you can walk a quarter mile along the bed of pine needles
that was Main Street before the storm surge, a few trees
in flower with odd magenta, somehow oriental, petals.
It's a kind of messy paradise, really, but
for the graveyard. The dead face east; the sun
that beads the morning sky, in haze or perfect blue,
must roll across the far gulf aground on this side
of the isle, their side. But all the island's theirs,
unless you count the eagles. I've seen their curved beaks
tear fishes from the ospreys' grasp. The high tide floats
my kayak through the inlet between rookery
and graveyard. I twirl the eyepiece for focus
in first light with the tide, the water surface sometimes
still as a looking glass, and I can see the oyster beds
and fish just as clearly as the bare-eyed blue herons,
sometimes jagged like an oil painting, look around,
and breathe the wild aroma of sand-muck, sea mammals,
lemon, salt, and grass. My lungs lift
as if I'd swallowed a small seabird and it took
the currents offered it and still flew. Improbable,
but something did stir, the way wind stirs
in a strange orchard, flicking a flower
we cannot stare quiet or less strangely gorgeous.

When I read the twenty chiseled names of the buried
families, factory workers, fishermen, and their wives,
no one else stood in the cedar grove, then voices
wafted down the path: a scene in a movie,
perhaps, and the island a painting by Winslow Homer.

Kayaking after Dusk

All the way back to the harbor
gray phosphorous and saffron as the night
comes on I keep turning to look for the island
in its lee in head winds

and look for furls beneath the water
of dolphin and scarcer shark as the west
blazes then shuts over the gulf

I paddle to the few lights after sunset
counterbalanced the hours
caught like baits till I and the water
and the sky are mixed as if the moment

I rinsed my mouth and spat
and the ocean was a jar for me to do this
I was a part of the tide and rocking

the dark comes over the water
and looking outward in that dark
is the same as looking inward

only the harbor stays apart and divisible
seeds on the black sill

the unforgetting seeds look
the harbor burns

Given

That the deck chair rocks in the wind
and paradisal light touches the gulls.
That the isle is enchanted, foams on waters.

Who are you to believe you are untrue
to yourself? Who must you be?

The breathing mouth and the whorled ears
will stop and indulgences of flesh,
sometimes a fever in the brain,
will melt like bread in water.

And body, brine on skin, all living fluids,
evaporate, fall back into island soil.
Faith and love into atoms without form and limb.
And the sun into darkness and into sun.

That the heart isn't really pure; too meager,
yes. That the gulls lift suddenly, simply,
and call out horror and sweetness, facts of our fate.

And day lasts longest here
by this part of the island by the orange tree . . .

EIGHT

Reap

Mother warned, "Don't catch a rabbit that will let you."
On the lawn, sides heaving, a small one wears illness like
a dirty coat. Bitten in its burrow by the sliding snake or
licked by the cold tongue of fastidious snows, now it's come
into the sun of the yard to die. Its eyes are liquid, bright,
but its mind is old. With its softly expressive fur
it moves the watching children and their parents. Does it
see its shadow, anything, hunched in the grass? Does it
know the last darkening where once it leapt and melted into
underbrush, changing lines of sight, twirling spectral
followers, magnificent in escape? It waits now in
blood and fur and flesh, or seems to, for someone or some-
thing to place the cage, the trap, hands, or teeth around it,
hot slow light threading away. It steals through its last garden,
legs weary, and is smoothed by the soft grays, as if with compassion.

How to Hunt

The deer vanish into the forest,
patches of red oaks,
a bumper crop of beechnuts and acorns.
You try to be as clean as possible.
Your hunting clothes are laundered
in no-scent detergent. You also shower
and shampoo with no-odor soap.
You stay downwind or use a cover scent.
Some people like fox or coon urine,
but you really prefer doe pee;
it seems natural when you're hunting deer
and has a calming effect on the whitetails.
Nothing is moving. Toward evening though
the deer should be up and feeding.
Dominant buck urine or fresh doe-
in-heat lure can attract the deer's attention
away from the hunter, so use it on scrapes
and in film canisters hanging from saplings
near your stand. The big eight-pointer
you've been watching all October
walks on and on outside your range,
but feed patterns change. The deer and turkey
have started to leave the meadows
to feed in the hardwoods. How rich the nut meat is
and how good, they taste. A northerly
wind picks up then settles and squirrels
like little freight trains
stop running in crisp leaves. It is so still
and the bowstring is pulled to your ear.
That's how to feel. Whatever comes
into the clearing must find its own way to outlast you.

Mr. Brink

In the magnolia the differing light
was of no consequence to Mr. Brink now
as he lay in the lower limbs. The wind
came from the east mornings as it had to
like a giant dove, pink and gray, and nothing
happened. Life was all but done;
it was as if Circe had married Mr. Brink
and their infant played in the ominous
shadows with sticks. The tree was *her* spell.
And as the sun rose and the wind died,
the loved who were lost or were won,
incurable, with honeycombed bones,
lay in the heat which threw up ash
like old starlight, and ash came down
around them. But their eyes flickered
still. A dog convulsed beneath a truck,
a cat could not leave off toying
with a spinning mouse, and beside the still
river, the ones with waxwork faces and skin
lay down again and again. The staining west,
nameless to Mr. Brink, meant no parting,
no leaning dark or dawning, until the spell
broke. See him step down from the twisted
gold branches and offer his chill hand
to the ancient infant, who grows invisible.
Circe-less, he steps forth onto the avenue,
a little heartsore, and the dove moans
in the heavens, renewing and ending sorrow.

NINE

Conch

Tubular eye extends. Can it see out of water?
Claw levers. Then with a swilling jelly
sound
the animal swells, as a sponge does,
wettened. This creature has its own supply
of wet;
for that we dislike it.

Think what it can make of our fingering
odor.
Bubbling, it retracts
and like a flowerhead in nighttime
holds its closed shape,
which insinuates then grapples:
belle-laid.

I took it for the shell,
and having seen its discrete death, a slow
crawling
(hitching)
over stones toward the lapping waves,
I value it the more;
hold the sculptured mouth to an ear,

and the ocean remembers
for me its drenched sound,
current and drift and beads of mist;
take it away
and dark waters run away from me:
minus body, perfect
as souvenir.

It was late in the day but I saw what flicked in his eye,
secret humor and horror, a way to live in god's eye,

I thought, the man at the marina telling of the sheer
number of stingrays in shallows mating. O brilliant eye

to perceive no stranger creature in the dappled water.
Jellied sea hares also swim beneath the sun's copper eye;

krill, sand dollar, sea anemone, blow fish, and oyster
mate in season, salt swishing, in the blinking of an eye.

Do they feel their longing, is it in their skimming so close
to the bottom, and did *he* feel it? Was that in his eye?

Rays are spined and supple, and they have to be careful—
almost impossible to conceive their passions. But why?

It's all symbol, impossible to conceive pure passions—
joy, humor, the seven deadly sins, layered in the eye

as the ground is layered; when the light changes you catch it
briefly, but then another current shows up in the eye.

He asked me if I liked scallops, and he told me about
the fisherman, he hadn't believed it either, blank eye,

who showed how with a hammer and steel pipe a stingray's wings
could be punched into sweet scallops. I thought of the false eyes

on a butterfly's wings, of a giant preening butterfly,
the urine it sucks, and the bird's beak and obsessive eye.

How immense and how small the feeding world is, bits of flesh
and flora, and the sexual currents, nymph and mayfly

and imago emerging in sunshine, expendable
after an hour or a day in desire. We fly

like stingrays, in radiant waters of imagination.
There's no surfeit like ours, no beatitude greater than *I*.

Requin

If in memory a pulse of music swims
with the great white shark, what notes for autumn
withering, and what signature for ground

swell—slow, cerebral, or horns' crescendo?
To wear the white skin of the coming snow
and hear the palsied cries of finches, how

else to know absence? To hear ritardando
in ebbing tide, and ghosting red tones
in the dawn. As silence requires music,

so death requires requiem, a lyric
resting in the eternal: Shark
in French is *requin,* an allusion to

the silent white deadliness; consonants
for being, for swimming with a body
in the jaw, for the startling return

to darker tones after so much clear blue.
To become more clear-eared before nature.
Even Cézanne's last paintings of nature,

*Pistachio Tree at Château Noir, Mont
Sainte-Victoire,* in purifying whites make
the unheard world: silences before vows

sung under the breath, and after tone rows
of fresh wind in pistachio boughs.
Sunlight is ivory, locks of the artist's

fine hair, and you nearly can hear his voice
as he paints the mauve and white and moist
purple of mountains. Listen. Listen hard.

If you don't hear it, later on you will,
disguised with quiet, as requin is, with
that intensity of feeling, song, death.

TEN

Eel Spearing

Just before dawn a woman and boy have come
to the river, water all stir, boat bobbing
and softly slapping, and soon she is leaning forward

while he holds steady the boat. Where prickling brown
meets smooth shining brown in eddies, they watch
for the sinuous shadow of the eel beside a sunken rock.

The boy's face suffuses with a quiet glow,
and soon the breaking day will catch him, and us,
whose imaginations strain after the shape in the water,

in its purples and yellows—in a time made simple
by the motion of the waves rocking, filling in
the small depressions in the riverbank, smoothing,

mixing, and dissolving clots of earth. If any
are thirsty, they can cup hands and drink. For now
we all are looking into the dark stream and the darker

pools—under a spell, so when darning needles
and water walkers hop, then are flying, whichever
of them falling first falling to the frog who stirred

them up, we only see eel. The boat rocks,
the water almost opaque but for sun through alders
glancing off the crumpled surface in one breath

of wind, then sinking a foot or more, and it is
promise, tone, direction, regret, and love.
This is the power of their bodies, the woman's

and the boy's, and of the eyes, jars spilled
back into the river. She holds the spear.
Something moves and piles up.

The Gross Clinic

I have a sister who takes care of animals, whose artistry is flesh
and blood mixed in with a dream or more
she tries to give her son. He cuts school and drinks with his friends
in the scrub woods behind the school. He thinks he wants to be an architect;
he thinks the poems he writes are portions of his unmixed spirit.
His habits of mind aren't settled, ossifying so slowly for many of us,
we can't know, and no one can tell him anything about cigarettes,
bad drugs, his fragile mortal spiral.

He can't cry anymore—it's the wrong style of feeling—,
and he only half knows that like his mother he will have to descend
before he can break into nakedness, as if from the warmed surface
of loam, from slug-soft matter that breathes or suppurates.

My nephew Samuel has the same name as the son of the famous surgeon
Dr. Gross, painted by the American realist Thomas Eakins.
Samuel chugs gin, takes his tokes, and helps his mother with preps—
a Betadine swabbing, "like a ritual," out from the site of the incision.
He confuses his mother. In this poem I want to try to stand
at their shoulders in the clinic. I think I could come near to swooning
from the obscene odor in the air, but I can try to imagine
something beyond the surgery, the fur and the glistening
blood, and I wouldn't leave them.

The flight of gray gulls over the bay
accompanied my early wrestling with flesh, "Blue Suede Shoes"
playing on the radio in my parents' house.
The fluency, then, of hands and lips threw seeds of a sweeter
and more luxuriant fluency when I was thirty.

Then I believed in the beauty of Helen
and sometimes, as the fullest truth, in the colored clouds

69

above apple trees full of blossoms and the reddened fruit afterwards.
In the end, of course, the fruit turns to mash, and wasps
burrow drunkenly in the meat no longer crisp.

⬱

There is a terrible beauty in the speeches of Nestor
after Agamemnon has called out the spirit of his army
by inviting them to go home. Imagine the sober tones
of the generals and the old king, his face a lifelong gallery
of portraits, grizzled hair an aura, as he faces

them with his counsel. From his lips a kind of honey
mixing with the bitterness of those two quarreling.
He asks them for their mettle, earth born, and leans,
foreshortened, his robe exposing a scarred and whitened chest.

A vignette of what we cannot learn, or outlast.

⬱

One who loves earth and the sun and animals
stands over the necrotic thigh of a wolfhound
with scalpel and rongeur, a patina of antiseptic
reddening the bare skin around the wound. The odors are a mixture
of rotted flowers and fruit and the beautiful blood oozing from an incision
above a honeycomb of maggots, swollen, moving.
If you can bear to stand close and look closely at the dissection,
you will feel your own stomach turn and your nerves
grow a little cleaner, and you may feel puzzled how a person
would want to know that much anatomy.

Wasn't it like this for Michelangelo?
This lesson of body? And the artist's revulsion, someone trying
to look beyond the heroic contours of ruined flesh—
softness of hip and buttocks—into the serum of spirit?

To live while another no longer can live.
This flesh and that muscle, and tinted spring forests, and mausoleums.

Two anthills and a late summer hive
gone to fragments.
The dirt is acrid, the wax honeyed—
so mind makes laws, dividing seasons,
scents, light and light's reflections.
I have no mother. Yes, you have a mother,
a voice said. But that is not right. Her difference—
a broken hive . . . a black bear in the bluebells
clawing the stinging air . . . something torn from her.
Still, the land soothes me—*No one may come*—:
low sun, dusk, and charred trees,
seeming first to glow as they darken, really are only darkening,
as if autumn burned.
And if I want it otherwise, o self,
there's beauty in small lies.
I say bees lick nectar after dark
and bring it to the bough of the honey tree.
Royal jelly keeps the larvae from falling
from the cells. *Broodcomb, honeycomb, bee bread—*
this is a harmless thought. Yes, once I *had* a mother.
I said to her, There is no twenty
on the clock, don't worry. I said
I will tell you the time. She said how little it takes
to finish . . . *What?*
Stupid, orphean things swirl:
apricot flowers . . . bees circling
as many times as the distance to the nectar . . .
throbbing wings . . . buzzing . . .
then to pluck the mind from darkness
singing. Mother hears
ambient grief and, more and more,
her earlier German tongue—rhyming, Schiller lines.

Where were you? I'll ask. *Wer bist du,* she'll say,
winter in voices, drifting,
snow drift, freezing, the bees dropping
to the hard pan inner darkness . . . o mother . . .

ELEVEN

A Woman like Yourself

You walk toward a woman like yourself,
but older,
only she isn't. You know how that is?
It could be anywhere
(rue de Charpentier, maybe),
and as strong a desire not to die
as anything you've felt before
darkens in your nerves. You'd need stars
in the brain
to feel your own self.
You think, her friends, the bric-a-brac
in her dressing room, blouses, even a gesture
as her daughter turns her head
will outlast her presence here,
now, by an *épicerie*
with its signs and elaborate fruit boxes,
JUS DE POMMES POUR VOTRE SANTÉ,
another language, piece-bright,
to rinse and wring the ear.
Already around the next curve
of her way, the woman goes,
and the moment means nothing
that the mind doesn't magnify.
Aren't we too real
to be otherwise? You adjust
a strand of hair behind your ear,
perhaps a sigh, a rueful glance
at your reflection in the little spot of glass
free from advertisements.
Then in your ardor,
only yours, you resume
the day, lured by something,
but as if nothing at all
happened.

Hem of Sunlight

And then I closed my eyes
on dusty gold
and twilit skies.
A shadow, a margin, a cold
hem of sunlight,
were all that stayed, and not one trace
of color, no lamplight
in a window, nor face.
The darkness too will wrinkle and decay,
and all will rebegin
when dawn comes in,
I told myself to say
and then slept—no clear sense remained.
A full-finished garden
behind a gate, sun stained
and covered with lichen
rosettes, gold, gray, and pink-
brown, surreptitiously
grew. Voices from among tree rows
slapped the leaves then sank.
I knew only
their tones, one as if caught—
a stillness, a resistance, cool—
the other dark,
the way a dark
thread can unspool.
There were shadows
as plentiful as light;
the light was beetled in the trees;
the pliant trees
stood still.

A strange glory,
a sense of moment, so lovely
and intense, lingered over all,
and then it changed,

as we are changed.
A wind rose—I'll call it the wind—
and the lake figuring the sky
trembled. The sounds
of moving feet
on the whispering ground
and whimpers. Who doesn't nakedly fear
in the back of his mind,
on her head, chill-rushing,
what watches everywhere
and everything?
I am the fear
that frightens me,
the garden of despair,
the hunter and the hunter's ear,
I hissed or something hissed at me.
And then I sat upright.
It shone so, the walls malachite
greenly spilling
from sky and air.
It was nothing.
I felt no weight
setting the sun alight.
I was awake and it was sweet
when in the street
a truck began to stitch
the road. I heard the gears shift.

Hydrangeas

FOR DICK

After the woman was gone,
I was alone.
The anemone appeared
as always above the moist dirt;
dust and pollen lay like sheets
over tables and lampshades.
Desire came and went,
explaining nothing.
One night the house
was lit throughout by lightning,
the sky leonine,
wind and rain
roaring. But when I went
to close the windows,
I could only stand
looking out, my heart
was the house, and it seemed
her figure stood, too,
in the wet shadows,
like a marble nymph
come to life.
The world was green,
then dark again,
and her figure
in the hydrangeas
kept leaving, over and over,
a flaring of the moments between us,
her body with its weight honeyed,
with its salt and alkali,
hewed down a year ago
and now part of her earth,
the garden she put up
around us.

One Fine Day

I saw you leave and return. A bunting
sang "pity to sleep," and you were smiling;
the skies were creamy, the fruit not falling;
one hour, two hours ago.

Among cloud boughs and mists and singing
I walked, through vineyards, past stone walls ringing
Lavigny, and I heard no one call me.
Did you tell me you called me?

I heard you leave and return. Morning
was never more beautiful, life-in-death,
death-in-life, the plums just falling,
one hour, two hours ago.

About the Author

Carol Frost divides her time between Cedar Key, Florida, and upstate New York. Her poems have appeared in the Pushcart Prize anthology three different years, and she is the poetry editor for *Pushcart XXVIII*. She is also the recipient of two fellowships from the National Endowment for the Arts. Her books include *Love and Scorn, Venus and Don Juan,* and *Pure,* all published by TriQuarterly Books/Northwestern University Press.